THE LIKENESS

MARTHA KAPOS is an American transplanted in London. Her background was in the visual arts: training as a painter at the Chelsea School of Art, and subsequently teaching there in the History of Art Department until her retirement in 2000. Since then she has been Assistant Poetry Editor at *Poetry London*. *My Nights in Cupid's Palace* (Enitharmon, 2003) was a Poetry Book Society Special Commendation and won the Aldeburgh First Collection Prize, and her second, *Supreme Being* (Enitharmon, 2008), was a Poetry Book Society Recommendation.

Martha Kapos

THE LIKENESS

ENITHARMON PRESS

First published in 2014
by Enitharmon Press
10 Bury Place
London WC1A 2JL

www.enitharmon.co.uk

Distributed in the UK by
Central Books
99 Wallis Road
London E9 5LN

Distributed in the USA and Canada
by Dufour Editions Inc.
PO Box 7, Chester Springs
PA 19425, USA

ISBN: 978-1-907587-39-9

Enitharmon Press gratefully acknowledges the financial support of
Arts Council England, through Grants for the Arts.

British Library Cataloguing-in-Publication Data.
A catalogue record for this book is available
from the British Library.

Designed in Albertina by Libanus Press
and printed in England by
SRP

'Odd that a thing is most itself when likened'

RICHARD WILBUR

CONTENTS

HOMECOMING

i.m. S.V.

While we stood and raised our glasses
you stepped out of your clothes.
Your face slid from our thoughts as headfirst
you bowed and went deep
into the warm pond where the water

moves inevitably under its lid
still as a box and there you are
the same length as the water
whiskered and white, rolling onto your back
a sleepy dogfish basking along the bottom

where it's dark in the spacious mud
eyeing up the distant
undersides of algae and transparent green lily pads
the numerous flies pulling in tightly together
humming a low riff over the water

while Burl Ives comes in with
Jimmy crack corn and I don't care
under the hot clouds and long blue days of summer
when Florida was like no place on earth.

THE MAGNETIC FIELD

Aloof and entire on the pillow
your white-washed face lifted up
almost too high to reach

and all the cardinal points of your body
laid out on this bed we didn't make
became a silent spectacle

arranged on a bare mahogany table
at the back of a long hushed room at school
to teach us magnetism.

Pigeons tapping their heads in the yard
stems of grass, the small sunlit gravel
beyond the half-opened shutters

were stopped in the furious
speed of their lives until
statements of fact as slight

as the sound of cutlery on plates
heard from a distant window
were folded in around your hands

until tall blocks of cloud
edged forward to form an audience
until faint trails of skywriting

gathered in swathes and drew
the entire minor contents of Massachusetts
into a circumference

its patterned slopes and valleys
its airy streets
a paper napkin floating in a puddle

all stood arranged in a series
of fine concentric circles to petal
and fan from your head and feet.

LIKE NOTHING ELSE

It could have happened like this
– that his body took up its old position
at a distance like the big house

we'd known since childhood
but when we parked the car, no doors

threw themselves open
no room we ventured into was more
than the shadow of a room

– except that even the echoey air
inside the hollow privacy of a house

would not give an adequate account
any more than if the heavy coat
we'd discovered massed in a heap

in the corner had been buttoned
tightly around nothing, any more than if

his body stood amongst apple trees
behind the house and we'd witnessed
a beheading – a piece of fruit

knocked loose from its stem had dropped
into a bucket – except that even

such an extreme account falls short
of the way his body persevered
in emptiness, as if the bundled outlines

of a sketch had been rubbed out
mark by mark until the page was blank.

AERIAL PERSPECTIVE

We're scanning the horizon to find your likeness
in the thin retreating overlapping blues
that used to be these definite hills

before their green became the colour of air.
We send our eyes to hold them back
in case they step too close to the veering edge.
Even the stone buildings of that pointed village
are at risk. On the weightless steeple

there's a clock face we can no longer read
then we lose the clock and finally the church
out of which only the emphasis of a face
is looking back hovering and oval

like the surface of a spoon
with nothing left to spoil the impression
of the endless things you might become.

AS IN A PAINTING BY CLAUDE

His body had that same
unclear border with the air

a white blur mumbling a ghost
while I stood on a grand slope

in the middle distance – a feathery oak
silhouetted in all its detailed leaves

pushing back the river, the fishermen, the boat
the floats from which the net hangs

in a series of black dots linking
the boat with the distant shore

– it must have been a long time
before my eye came up behind me

and ran ahead, stopped to peer
as if hesitating at the parted foliage

the bare hills airing their gaps
then stretched out rippling and horizontal

into the final judgements of tone
yellowy blue and silvery blue almost inaudible

so that even if his body had escaped
entirely into air it would only be

because he was somewhere else
in the gathering dusk of the picture.

THE LIKENESS

after Marguerite Yourcenar

When broad as daylight you
became very gradually small
surely this was the greatest diminution.

As the ancient Chinese treatise
advised a novice
tackling the anonymous pale blue hills:

distant trees have no leaves
distant men have no eyes

but in this new place a long way off
where stones are mistaken for sheep
where your face is a pool of lively dots

a mob of birds across a nacreous sky at night
a black satellite picture of Norfolk wearing
a necklace of sprinkled beads

your hair, your hands, your smile evoke
someone I adore. Who? Yourself.

EYE

I looked for your eye. I looked
for any light at all staring

from the body's long house at night
where it lay stretched out

full length between trees, its grey roof shut
its impenetrable dark back turned

and I imagined from the other side
I'd see your very wide lit face

its innumerable yellow rooms

two children playing
their light heads together laughing.

FATHER WILLIAM

With so much going on outside
you forget how the world
feeds itself into a tiny hole

in the eye, tunnels its way
to a back room and stands on its head.

You forget how the brain
admitting its mistake, tips it back
onto its feet, connects

the very small to the very large
and tidy housekeeper that it is
stacks it all in strict
time sequence in the linen cupboard

where now, after so many blunders
the shelves have collapsed and the sleek
sheets scattered by the wind

have changed their names and become so small
lightly floating flying across the front lawn –

a dandelion stands on its head
and its hair has become very white.
The unfastened minutes trickle out

until the past is a wisp
lodged in some ditched bicycle
face down on the pavement, or the wrecked
spectacles you've left on the table.

THE TOP

Given to me larger than life
it stood up almost motionless
screaming its would-be music

then with a light jump
started out across the wide

grey square of linoleum
with every intention of cutting
a deep highway through the house.

Mounted on one toe
as if it was a fixed idea

the solitary king of a vacant
three hundred and sixty degree kingdom
flinging circles all the way out

to their apogee, it tempted gravity
by leaning headlong

almost to the point of falling
then vertical and defiant
raced to its own emergency singing

That bitch doesn't know who's boss
mixing its rainbow colours in the wind.

Even though it was a work
much smaller than the human body
there was nothing to stop it

knocking down its own father and mother
a steel-eyed presence

with a profile inverted
like the cone of a tornado
and a nose as towering

as the nose of a Roman emperor
the one whose appointed slave

trailed at his heels
bearing the constant reminder
– *You are only human.*

AS HE SEES HIMSELF

I

A single tree stricken and small stands
between himself and the great Atlantic.

Whatever the tree tells him he is – he is.

If he sees it gripped by the wind
his shaggy arms elongate, struggle and bend.

If its branches are flung into the air
his eye runs out to their snapped dead ends

their wishbone twigs and disappears.
If he sees its stubborn trunk leaning

but in no hurry to go anywhere, his legs
stiffen and push through their shoes.

Soon he is far out on a limb where a few
of his words are left. A hand drops

his hand and a detached leaf falls
small to the point of indifference.

Hang there like fruit, my soul, till the tree die.

II

A single tree stricken and small stands
between himself and the great Atlantic.

The smooth humped mass of ocean takes
all the time in the world

slowly lifting blue and dark blue
into a backdrop in the distance.

One day, when the wind got up, he saw
a picture assemble itself

as easily as light when it picks out
each indifferent thing and spills

the entire contents of a room into colour.
The tree seemed to produce

a scattering of buds, their white caps blowing
violent and alive. Or was it only

some flakes of foam loosened by the wind
sweeping past the running branches

in a fleet of lights? His body stood
arms out and flowered along its length

while in his leaning shade, his peeled eye
took in both the Atlantic and the tree.

SHE DRESSED HIM ENTIRELY

Taking it down from the hook
with panoramic holes for his head and arms
she dressed him entirely

in the present moment, the confirming
yes to everything he said
tucking him up in bed, smoothing

the sheets, laying out the views
from the window: all the shapes
she made of the blue-green

grapevine hung over the garage
the sumac with its many-budded spikes
placed on the curving lawn

so that he proceeded among them
into the deep garden where trees
displayed their new collections of leaves

each waving a long stem towards him
holding a lozenge of green light
as if they were extensions of his own eye

and the sky stood open in motionless
pieces of shining the size of a diamond.
Her face in its largeness swam

on a repeating wave of arrival
coming as it did from a place
where the sun sat on his bed as if

it would never move, never go into eclipse
behind the sliding shadow of a door
or ever give up its shape and grow thin.

THE ICE HOUSE
on lines by Edward Thomas

Temperature has a terrible way
with water, taking your breath hostage
locking a quick flood in a jar.
The pond behind the ice house is frozen
as if cast in a spell. Out early
you cannot see your own feet
for the opaque white mist that hangs
suspended over the ice.

'But not so long as you live
Can I love you at all.'

Touch on this subject
very lightly in case you fall through.
Step lightly. Step as lightly as hands
running over a face
rotating past the same numbers
without striking the time.

Look down as you walk across:
the ice exhibits its transparent past.
Surviving one spring after another
trapping stems, blades, buds –
a loss is held marooned inside a loss.

A replica world makes a sound
like a groan or applause under your feet.

STARTING PISTOL

Drawn into itself
a word is a thin

shaft of vision
that narrows

its shoulders
to aim

dead straight
for the hills.

But in the hope
of finding you

in deep focus
in front of me

standing arms out
where I can see you plainly

your dimensions
framed and discrete

I am trying to
hold back the long

discursive lines
from flying out

from racing after
one another in paler

and paler sequence.
I am trying to

string out
on my breath

certain floating words
before I find

they've disappeared
beyond earshot

into the quick
past tense of go.

THE SILENT COLOUR

Words say one thing but tell
me again about that particular green
all lustre and light and apart –
unpronounced in a place just before

the mouth is opening its lips
before words disperse it completely
among 'and' and 'and' and 'and'.

Let me continue to see it standing
at the desired angle like you

resting your weight on one leg
in the kitchen sunlight as if you were
an apple tree in the field of vision

if an apple tree with its meticulous fingers
could prepare a green salad
of fennel, avocado and the juice of tangerines
and open a bottle of white wine.

ORDNANCE SURVEY

I have examined you in my mind.
The background looks vaguely like the sea off Dartmouth
but you are smiling at me, as you proudly
hold out two parasol mushrooms.

I expect you to increase your wide farm-boy smile
delicately smiling your face into more lines
than we'd see in the evening walking out
under raking light across ploughed fields
deeply incised with shadows.
The question is how to survive the long
furrows and dark stubble sliding
down one hill, rising on the next
until they are finally pinching closed
in a speck on the horizon.

They are gathering momentum as my eye
attempts to hold them still
as a map showing the flat footpaths of South Hams.

THE INVENTION

This colour will invent your last smile
swept up into a rattling heap
of leaves. This very brown

discovered by a random wind
is your exact presence on the threshold
blown in from the night

and, as if long hidden under the dry
noise of my tongue
a word had been forming there and waiting

for me to swing open the door
to find you spreading your arms, triggering
the security light

it concentrates you
standing there
out loud, fully lit and smiling.

VENUS

Troubled, irregular
among clouds
then unfurling in the air
bright and bright

it's like a rope
snaking out
over choppy water
to find a place to tie up

it's like a cabin
precise and white
at the end of a long walk
through thick Prussian pines

it's like a window
whose solitary bulb
holds out hope
on a late black empty street

it's the one shy word
crossing your lips
like a man appearing in a doorway
who has come home.

THE OPEN ROAD

In one direction
it goes straight
to its end
giving its life
to a pinpoint
endlessly making
an end of it
on the horizon.
You could be fooled.
One minute it seems
to lie flat on a hill
the next it gets up
and curves
cheerfully taking
everything with it
around a bend.
No matter you always
want to know
what happens next.
It's a poor hero
of slender means
playing hell
with your expectations
a thin procession
snaking
in both directions
unable to distinguish
in front from behind.
If it had eyes
like Janus on both sides
of its head
it wouldn't know
which way to look.

Tears roll out
of its tear-ducts into
its well-supplied drains.
You keep your headlights on
in the rain.
If you try to turn back
there's only
a jot or a freckle.
As you get close
an irregular
white spot hovers
between trees
and a shape
assembles itself into
your vague home.

The House

House on a missed turning –
not so far away
as the unseen spaces latent
in blocks of stone
but deep as the brains
of animals whose smooth
fur heads you can feel
right under your hand
or perhaps, more like the distant
fish at the bottom of a pond
whose glinting movements
you can see twirling the water
without seeing the fish
we have gone on a long way
without a moment
of looking back to this or that
lost street wondering whether
in a room at the back
with tall windows thrown open
to a commotion of trees
we would have sat together
in a play of light and shade
speaking or silent.

The Thread

Say it starts when her mother stood
like a door with its back turned
in a huff. And below among the patches
of remaining snow are the silent
concrete steps, a wintery
ribbon of road, a thread, a string
'an apron string', she says to herself.

A path almost erased
by the white intervening winters
lies down behind a succession of hills
an acute diminution of perspectives
until a house standing on the top
of the final hill looms

so large it reminds her of the way
the spool of thread stood
jumping and unwinding on the top
of the iron sewing machine her mother
pedalled hard to make a green
pattern grow out of white.

Word for a House

The word that strange muscle
the tongue makes for a house appearing
then vanishing from sight
behind the profile of a hill

tries to catch it like a path
in hot pursuit
begging, worn palm upwards
empty-headed, empty-hearted

smaller, to and fro, then winding
smaller than it was before that

until it gives the distant
impression of light repeatedly
hitting a door to make it blush.

The Doorway

Thinner, almost a thread, the long intricate thought
a child strings between lost and home
somewhere, out of nowhere, it begins.

Her mother hesitating, then turning in a doorway
marks the spot a path began to pull away
roll down the avenues, flash
ahead between trees.
The huddled hills moved
apart to let it through.

Look quickly. Each new moment
winds it out
past the ancient house
the copper beech, the elephant rock
directly into her ear
where she's been waiting all her life
for the word to find her.

Current Page

A sheet of paper
the shape of a rectangle
is calling me back

to a door
as if it is a memory
but one I cannot actually remember

then turning her back
with a slam
as if her back is a door
but one I cannot actually open

I'm putting on speed
down a road
in the high hope

a word on a sheet of paper
the shape of a rectangle
is calling me back.

THE FIREPLACE

Nothing moves except a pulse
among the coals, an animation, a flickering
no more explicit than a red

among the black dilapidated scenes
grouped unsaid on a shelf
at the back of her mind

until inside the noiseless house
lit among the baby pictures
grey with dust and the small

bodies of flies
a life scarcely stronger than theirs
appears among the deaths.

Little one, little one, where is your voice?
O Mother, it belongs to the wind.
                    – Old Song

– *Look we are here!* they say from an inside room
lit and warm as a safe.

These are the distinct houses, the happy
life-sized ones of firm construction, the brick forts
whose blunt walls stand flush
with unassailable authority on the ground.

Perfect sentences unfurl in rapid streams
across the air: the mother-tongue of the house.
They flap their names like flags from the front door.

– *Little pig, little pig,* the wind blows up the steps
let me come in.

– *But you have only to knock.*

Knocking does not suit the feral style of the wind.
It blows in search of another house with thinner skin
one that resembles a shadow left sideways on the ground.

One it can make suddenly into a house so badly built
a breath shows a brief circle on a window
like the smallest thing said.

– *Little pig, little pig,* the wind blows up the steps
let me come in.

Half rain, half twilight, the wind lets itself in
through a missing slate.
It slips under a sash raised one inch.
Nothing more than a draft it fills the curtains out

until they balloon into shaky clouds
that have stepped unexpectedly into the room.
Delicately as air the long-winded wind
lifts the edges of the house and folds them back.

It pays close attention to the boundaries of in and out
the holes and notches even on the stem of a straw.

A breath inhabits the house pushing
a long opening inside it until
the ringing space is boned and hollow as a flute.

– *I'll huff and I'll puff,* says the wind

releasing a key
with the pressure of a fingertip.

NEWBORN

Light little moon face alone
in your vast cot and me
turned and called on the tide

your cry governs
with the force of gravity.
Your open moon mouth
bending me in one direction
forms an eager O in the dark.

And here we both see
the tender branches thread into the room
the walls collapse and dissolve.
The green released through the ceiling
enter the room in a flood.

In a clear string of syllables
the milk comes winding down
in waves with a wind blowing across them.
And these are the first words
ever spoken, the unstoppable sounds

the dazzle felt in the mouth filling it
as sun fills the room
solid as a hand held in a hand.

ASTRONOMY

For Isla on her birthday July 7 2011

At this chosen place it stepped from the earth
where a girl was sleeping among the large
washed-out roses that papered her bedroom.

On the opposite wall a white seam of light
broke open and a path sprang out
pulled ahead and ran away

released into the wide diamond day.
And as I'm imagining its airborne career
detached from its orbit, not fully formed

setting out into space from the picture on my desk
of a girl aged ten in a Greek chiton holding
in one hand a shield and in the other a spear

I'm making nothing less
than the analogy between a girl and a planet.

ALL THE WHILE

Among shrinking islands
of late snow news comes

that very young grass
has arrived in epic
numbers at the front door.

It stands up all eyes
in the open air, crushed
blades almost too green

for belief given that December
had seen off every
trace of childhood sunshine

while in an inside room someone
pays a visit to a girl
the moment she sees a wrinkled

woman standing in the mirror
and thinks
when did that happen.

AT THE HOUR SLEEP LOVED HER

such delicate and tender sleep
folded my mother and she lay
unminded and unbereaved
in some deep valley

even as if sleep had arms
to pick her up, even as if sleep

round and white
held her in a bowl
placed on a table long prepared
where the continuous feast was milk.

EROS AT WIMBLEDON

The big topspin forehand
flops at the net. Set point
a doubtful call, a failed return

the rising and falling mood.
Once more the ball girls and boys

scamper to collect the strays.
But now it is true: we are transfixed

by the merciless perfection of a ball
placed just inside the line

brought agog to our feet
gaping like the open flap of a tent
or a baby bird swallowed

in avid submission
by its own huge pleading mouth.

NORWAY

This deep apple eatable
yet unable to be eaten

is standing upright on a plate.
The stout flesh and pips only inches

from my teeth and tongue, yet as remote
as someone in the white interior

of a clapboard house standing on a hill
prominent and alone

under storm-light and tall opulent clouds
in a northern landscape bordering on the sea

perhaps in Norway.
But look! My mouth widening

to its maximum extent
can take in the whole of Norway.

LAKE TANTALUS

As if someone has come shining to find me
the lake extends in my direction
its oval surface like a brimming spoon.

The water shivers slightly.
Upside-down the broken reflections show
a wall of high grass, a white house
you can't quite see from the road
a bowl of sugar on a table
pushed back too far to reach.

      The lake looms closer like someone
      coming for entire decades
      to find me, inching forward
      in intense sunlight and bringing
      every full drop by degrees

      all the more slowly away.
      Receding from all that light
      the blue water framed in pines
      seems to hover in a doorway like someone
      turning to reach for a coat.

What do I make of the repeated
pattern of retreat? The ebbing
ripples making endless
understatements lapping in, lapping in
the inaudible bubbles like someone
suppressing a yawn.

What's going to happen here is goodbye
except that, never completely
turning away, the lake goes back for miles

on a long promise
like a man who has two arms
and keeps them folded across his chest.

THE PRIVATE LIFE OF THE TONGUE

At home unfathomable and secret
it had reasons of its own
tucked into a single bed behind closed doors

in the individual loneliness of his mouth.
For long periods in the afternoons
it would contract itself and draw in

unable to lengthen, reach over and open the curtains.
Did the room have a frescoed ceiling?
Attendants bowing and sliding backwards

in anticipation of *le grand lever*?
The word she wanted to hear
speaking to her alone: she imagined it

on the shiny tip of his tongue,
a mahogany piano standing upright in a corner
superior and dark, its great lid shut

as Mozart waited lightly on the keys.
In all probability it had no more
to do with her than a chapel in the woods

whose altar with its one dry candle
had remained unvisited for years.
Never mind if it lay there dreaming

of the ritual of tucking in, the kiss goodnight.
She knew it would settle back to the shapes
it had taken in its other lives remembering

how it played havoc in a young boy
lying with its steaming pink root exposed
on a large plate in the kitchen

or hanging out a very red red
from the mouth of a black dog
it was impossible to avoid on his way to school.

ALBERTINE'S MOLE

When her face lies open, fast asleep
sometimes at night I'm the unrequited lover

peering down and taking in the view.
Her profile meandering sideways

on the pillow draws a craggy sunlit line
of curves and inlets such that could divide

the eastern seaboard of the United States
from the Atlantic: providing proof

I'd like to think, against the slightest risk
of continental drift except that floating

within the radius of her cheek
(as if an intruder, having tiptoed in at night

had disturbed the established order on my desk)
a small brown mole is slowly changing its position.

As it settles now in one uncertain place
and then another, shifting its location

depending on mine, the distant spot
is a remote but sizeable town perched high

on a chalky slope above the harbour
or from another angle, closing in, it's a single

farmhouse by an adjoining pond where, settling softly
a little to the left, a concentration of gnats

dips down to practise landings on the water.
Freckled shadows fall from the surrounding trees.

In the general darkness I can just make out a man
and, unless I'm very much mistaken, he's bending down

to toss a small round stone into the water.
Rings fan out and leave me circling

in the baffling echoes of her whereabouts
where for all I know the story peters out

until at last I spot it sinking down
through clouds of watery bottle-green so dark

my anxiously attentive eye flicks on
a torch as if her face was full of rooms

each one a prior world she'd passed through
and I track it down the unlit flights of stairs

back to the ultrasound department in the basement
where I'm an unexpected witness to the scan.

It's a transparent fish in the inky dark
a primordial shrimp whose neck is slit

with vestiges of gills, a lugworm
curling sideways in the mud, and deeper still

a small round beating shadow
the radiographer assures me is her heart.

A TRUE ACCOUNT OF TALKING TO THE SUN
IN PARKHOLME ROAD
after Frank O'Hara

'You told me trees pick up again
where they've left off –
but now, without their leaves
they have such a look of naked
emaciation that their hard
curves and hollows stand out like ribs
on the bare chest of Buddha.
And that Japanese Maple now bent and stiff
under a slick of white-out ice
left off last fall with an exceptional red
they'd said on *Gardeners' Question Time*
was a distinct sign of stress.'

                            'Be patient'
said the Sun, loud and clear
as it stepped in through the window.
'You know what an act of faith it takes
to believe I'll put in a reliable
appearance in the morning?

                            Well –
I'll not measure out any more distress
than you'll need to write your poems.'

'Can I be certain of that?' I asked.
'Not always', said the Sun.

ACKNOWLEDGEMENTS

Thanks are due to the editors of the following publications where these poems, sometimes in earlier versions, first appeared: *London Magazine, The Poetry Review, The Dark Horse, The North, The Times Literary Supplement*.

NOTES

Page 5:
Aerial Perspective is the term used for the way atmospheric conditions alter our perception of objects in the distance by causing them to lose colour and definition. Leonardo called it 'The Perspective of Disappearance'.

Page 7:
'The Likeness' has two lines quoted from Marguerite Yourcenar's *Fires* (1936).

Page 12:
In 'As He Sees Himself' *Hang there like fruit, my soul, till the tree die* is from *Cymbeline*, Act V, scene v. Tarkovsky's film *Sacrifice* initially provided the image of the tree.

Page 38:
In the *Odyssey* Homer described Tantalus as suffering in the underworld from unappeased hunger and thirst, while at the same time being immersed in water up to his chin.

Page 42:
'Albertine's Mole' is inspired by a passage from Proust in *Remembrance of Things Past*, 'In fact, whenever I saw her I noticed that she had a mole, but my inaccurate memory made it wander about the face of Albertine, fixing it now in one place, now in another.'

Page 44:
'A True Account of Talking to the Sun in Parkholme Road' refers to Frank O'Hara's 'A True Account of Talking to the Sun on Fire Island' together with Isak Dinesen's 'The Young Man with the Carnation' from *Winter's Tales* (1993).